Just Like You!

EMMA S. ROUNDTREE, PH.D.

ILLUSTRATOR: JAMES C. THOMAS

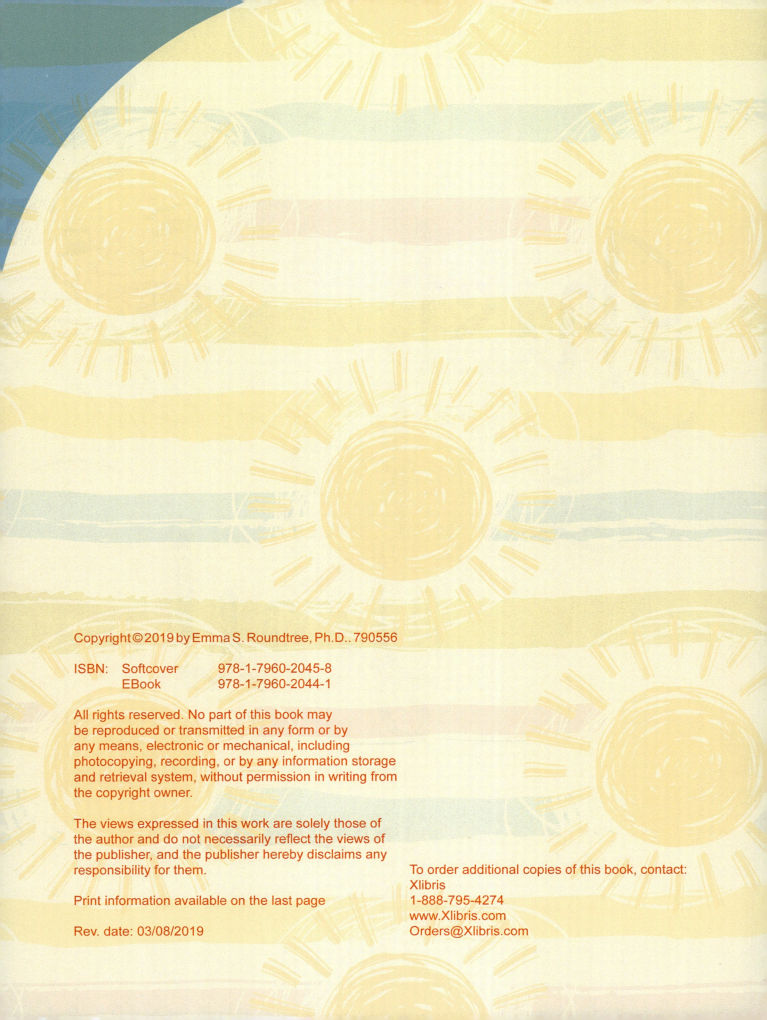

To order additional copies of this book, contact:
Xlibris
1-888-795-4274
www.Xlibris.com
Orders@Xlibris.com

TABLE OF CONTENTS

IN MEMORY OF ALEXIS PHILLPS

This book is written in memory of Alexis Phillips. She is one of my former students with disabilities. Although she was physically disabled, she had tons of personality. I considered her to be the extra adult in the classroom because she would give this look like, "You know Ms. Emma don't play that! You better get it together and quick!" LOL! She was a ball of joy and full of love for people she knew. A wonderful child that love meeting other children. If she could talk she would definitely hold a good conversation! We Miss you Lexi and rest in peace and love!

Disability

Many people like to refer to my condition as a disability. I really don't like it. They make it seem as if the way I am is a bad thing. I love to hear people refer to my condition as my ability. This a more accurate representation of who I am. My abilities hi-lights the things I can do and do well. Just like you have some things that you can do better than others, so do I. I am just like you!

Ask me my name

Hi! I have a name just like you. Ask me my name and I may use different ways to tell you. I may use an audible device. I may sign it out for you. I may write it down for you. I may even simply say it so you would know. Ask me my name and I will tell you. I am just like you!

Speaking

Stop speaking to me as if I am a baby!! I may have physical disabilities but my mental capacity may be well above average. Speak to me as if I am one of your other friends. I like to hear funny stories. I may not be able to talk back but I can definitely laugh. I am just like you!

Toys!!

I like toys, just like you! I may like to play in the sand or I may like to play in a box of crayons. The only difference is, I may not like the way things may feel or sound. You may not like that either. I am just like you!

Food

Oh, do I like the taste of food, just like you! It makes my stomach feel nice and full and I am very comfortable then. The only thing is, I may not like the different textures of all foods so I am really selective. But if I don't like it, I won't be rude and say "It's nasty" or "I don't like it", I just won't eat anymore. But, I am just like you!

Learning

I can learn new things everyday, just like you! The only difference is, I may not learn it as fast as you. It may take me a year to learn my alphabets and two years to learn my numbers. But, I can learn them and I will, just like you!

Environment

I am always striving to learn my environment. I may not get it right the first time and I may even get lost. But I am learning it just like you. I love seeing all the lights and signs telling me where things are. These things help me to travel the community safely. I am learning new things about my community each and every day. My environment at home and at school teach me all these things. But just like any other kid, I am just like you!

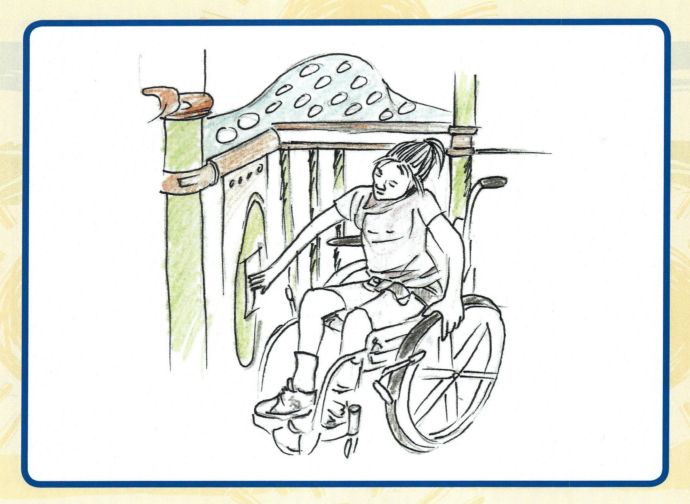

Music

Mussssiiiccc!! Oh, how I love music! Music makes me dance and feel all good inside. But sometimes, the pitches in the music and the sound of the instruments clashing may irritate my senses and I may not be able to withstand it. I may cover my ears up. I may even scream sometimes because it is too much for my senses to process. But, I'm just like you. I like music and I may even want to dance with you!

Sounds

Sometimes when I am nervous, I can't hide it. You may see me flapping my hands and moving around or even rocking back and forth. I am just trying to process the many sensory inputs I am receiving all at once. Have you ever been to a football game and everyone around you got really excited and started blowing horns and clashing sticks together? Do you remember how you didn't like that sound? Well, I experience that some times from some things that may not be that loud. But, I am just like you, I like to have peace within myself and sometimes those sounds disrupt my peace. I am always striving for peace. I am just like you!

Behaviors

I have a condition and sometimes that condition causes me to be physically aggressive. But I want you to know that my intentions are never to hurt you. I know my behaviors are not always acceptable and I am trying to learn new ways to show my anxiety and my frustrations. I know that you may be frightened of me and you may think that I may hit you, but if that ever happens please know that I am not trying to harm you. I am not trying to make you afraid around me. I want you to be comfortable around me. I am having to learn different ways to show my discontentment so please bare with me. Remember, I am just like you!

Teachers

Teacher! Teacher! Teacher! Please take the time to learn me! I am not like any other student that you have met. I have different needs and they are specific to me. I need you to learn how to treat me and to learn how to teach me. I want to be the best person that I can be. I want to possibly live independently one day. I don't want to depend on my parents and friends and other family forever. I need you to teach me the skills so that I can be as independent and successful as possible. Teacher, please remember that even though you only see some low points right now, there are some great things within me that can be built. I am depending on you to discover those things and teach them. Remember that one day,

I'll be just like you!

Parents

Mom and Dad, thank you! Thank you! Thank you! You two mean the world to me. I know I don't have the best way of showing it, but please know that I am very grateful for everything you have done. Remember, God placed us in each other's lives for a specific reason and we will be great together! Thank you for loving me and caring for me and nurturing me. One day I hope to be great parents JUST LIKE YOU!!

Glossary

Definitions for these terms were retrieved from webster.com

Disability: a physical, mental, cognitive, or developmental condition tat impairs, interferes with, or limits a person's ability to engage in certain tasks or actions or participate in typical daily activities and interactions.

Ability: The quality or state of being able.

Physically: In respect to the body.

Audible: heard or capable of hearing

Device: a piece of equipment or a mechanism designed to serve a special purpose or perform a special function

Capacity: an individual's mental or physical ability

Representation: the state of being represented

Sensory: Relating to sensation or to the senses

Textures: The visual or tactile surface characteristics and appearance of something.

Environment: The circumstances, objects or conditions by which one is surrounded.

Striving: to devote serious effort or energy

Withstand: To stand up against; oppose with firm determination.

Nervous: Easily excited or irritated.

Clashing: To come into conflict; to make a clash

Physically Aggressive: Physical contact that may cause harm (Dr. Roundtree's definition)

Grateful: appreciative of benefits received

Specific: restricted to a particular individual, situation, relation or effect

Nurturing: the sum of the environmental factors influencing the behaviors and traits expressed by an organism.

Printed in the United States
By Bookmasters